21st-century SCIENCE

NEW MATERIALS

Present knowledge • Future trends

Written by Robin Kerrod

W

FRANKLIN WATTS
LONDON · SYDNEY

This edition 2007

First published in 2003 by Franklin Watts

Copyright © Franklin Watts 2003

Franklin Watts
338 Euston Road
London NW1 3BH

Franklin Watts Australia
Level 17/207 Kent Street
Sydney NSW 2000

A CIP catalogue record for this book is
available from the British Library.

Dewey number 620.1'1

ISBN 978 0 7496 7384 0

Printed in China

Franklin Watts is a division of Hachette
Children's Books, an Hachette Livre
UK company.

Design Billin Design Solutions
Editor Constance Novis
Editor in Chief John C. Miles
Art Director Jonathan Hair
Picture Research Diana Morris

Picture credits
John Carter/SPL: 33
Fred Dott/Still Pictures: 11
David Drain/Still Pictures: 36, 37
Robert Garvey/Corbis: 10
Klaus Gulbrandsen/SPL: 6-7, 17
Jan Hinschl/SPL: front cover c, b cover,
4-5, 38, 39
Robert Holmgren/SPL: front cover bl, 27
Klein/Hubert/Still Pictures: 35
Lester Lefkowitz/Corbis: front cover t, 1, 2-3, 12
G. Muller/Struthers GMBH/SPL: 15
NASA: 29
National Maritime Museum, London: 31
Maurice Nimmo/FLPA/Corbis: 9
Alfred Pasieka/SPL: front cover bc, 34
Ray Pfortner/Still Pictures: front cover br, 40, 45,
46-7, 48
Antonia Reeve/SPL: 28
Harmut Schwarzbach/Still Pictures: 41
SPL: 18
Sporting Pictures (UK) Ltd: 22
Andrew Syred/SPL: 24, 25

Contents

Introduction   **8**

Raw materials   **10**

Marvellous metals   **14**

Polymers and plastics   **18**

Fibres and composites   **22**

Adhesives and superglues   **24**

Ceramics and glass   **26**

Clever crystals   **30**

Super silicon   **32**

Fuels for the future   **34**

Manipulating molecules and genes **36**

Materials in space   **38**

Conservation and recycling   **40**

Glossary   **42**

Index   **44**

INTRODUCTION

About two million years ago our distant ape-like ancestors began to make tools by chipping bits from lumps of flint. They were taking a giant leap forwards for mankind by adapting the materials around them for their own benefit. Strangely, in our modern age, chips of silicon – a material chemically similar to flint – have also brought about a revolution that is transforming the way we live and work.

To a large extent, the way humankind has developed has depended on the kinds of materials people have used. Prehistoric peoples employed only the materials they found around them, such as stone and wood. We call this period of human history the Stone Age. Little metal was used because only a few metallic elements – such as gold and silver – are found as metals in the Earth's crust.

In about 3500 BC, people discovered how to smelt the minerals that they dug from the ground to make the metal bronze. And they learned how to shape metal into objects by casting. This period of history is known as the Bronze Age. Another leap forwards came when people discovered how to make iron, about 2,000 years later, and an Iron Age began.

The Industrial Revolution

The use of iron expanded dramatically in the 1700s, when better smelting methods came into use. Iron proved to be a suitable material for making the machines that launched the world into the Industrial Revolution. By the mid-1800s, an even better material – steel – was being mass-produced, and steel is still by far the most important material in use today. We use dozens of other metals too, both alone and as mixtures in alloys.

But now vying with metals in importance are plastics, which are produced from chemicals. They spearhead a vast range of synthetic materials used in every walk of life, from dazzling dyes to incredibly strong superglues.

New materials and new ways of producing and using old materials are constantly being introduced. Exciting developments are taking place in the processing of materials in space, for example. Among other things, this could result in better alloys for construction and more effective medicines.

Conservation and recycling

One worry, however, is that we are using up the Earth's resources too quickly to make the materials we need. That is why conservation and recycling of materials is so important. But in the long term, we might have to look to space for our essential raw materials. Much the same rocks and minerals are found elsewhere in the Solar System – on the Moon for example. And if we are in dire need, we might even have to resort to mining the asteroids – lumps of rock and metal found in our Solar System beyond the planet Mars.

▼

Early peoples developed tools and weapons from whatever materials were to hand. This picture shows a selection of flint arrowheads and cutting tools.

raw

MATERIALS

The raw materials we take from the world around us provide the starting point for the many thousands of different materials we use. The main raw materials are the rocks and minerals that we mine, or dig, out of the ground.

The Earth's crust is made from many kinds of rocks, which are in turn made up of many different minerals. Minerals are compounds consisting of two or more chemical elements combined together. Altogether there are about 90 chemical elements in nature. All the millions of compounds in the world around us – our different materials – consist of varying combinations of just these 90 elements.

In addition, scientists have now developed about 20 artificial elements that do not exist in nature. They make these by bombarding elements like uranium with atomic particles. Many of these elements have proved useful.

Metal processing

Most elements are metals, for example iron and nickel. Non-metallic elements include solids such as carbon and sulphur, and gases such as oxygen and hydrogen. Most elements are not found in a pure form on Earth because they react, or combine with, other elements too readily. Instead, they are found as compounds, as in minerals. The elements have to be extracted from their compounds by chemical processing.

By far the most important compounds are the minerals known as ores. These are the rocks from which metals can be profitably extracted. Magnetite and haematite are two major ores of iron. They are iron oxides – compounds in which iron is combined with oxygen. Iron is extracted relatively easily by heating the ores with coke in blast furnaces, a process known as smelting.

But sometimes the extraction of metals from ores can be much more complicated. Take nickel, for example. A lengthy sequence of crushing, chemical flotation, magnetic separation, roasting, smelting, and finally electrolytic refining is needed to extract the metal. This process also results in the recovery of valuable amounts of silver.

Chemical raw materials

The minerals we dig from the ground also provide us with an enormous variety of chemicals.

Some, like talc, we can use as they are, while others are merely the starting point for a host of different products, such as soaps, acids and fertilisers.

The wood from trees is still one of our major materials for building houses and making furniture, and we shred it to make paper. But it is also a source of chemicals, from which we can make plastics and explosives.

The oceans and even the air provide us with raw materials as well. The oceans contain vast quantities of dissolved minerals, which is why they taste salty. The air is made up of a mixture of gases, such as nitrogen and oxygen. Most of these gases can be utilised in one way or another.

◄ ◄

This picture shows opencast (surface) iron-ore mining in progress at Mt Whaleback in Australia.

▼

An offshore production platform extracts oil – a vital raw material – from beneath the seabed.

raw materials

Petroleum refineries process crude oil into fuels and a host of useful chemicals.

Fossil fuels

Artificial (synthetic) materials such as plastics now rival metals in importance. But they are not produced from the rocks and minerals of the Earth's crust. They are manufactured from chemicals, obtained mostly from the so-called fossil fuels – petroleum, natural gas and coal.

These substances are called fossil fuels because they are the remains of living things that flourished on Earth hundreds of millions of years ago.

Petroleum, for example, is believed to have formed from organic matter – mainly plankton and simple plants – which built up in the sediment at the bottom of ancient seas. The matter began to decompose, or rot, and then increasing temperature and pressure converted the rotting matter into oil. Over time the source rock became compacted, and the oil was squeezed out. It slowly migrated to nearby porous rock, such as sandstone, where it collected in vast quantities.

Oil and gas are made up almost entirely of compounds of hydrogen and carbon, called hydrocarbons. Similar carbon compounds can also be obtained from coal by chemical processing. These compounds are termed organic, because all living organisms are made up of compounds based on carbon.

Coal tar

English chemist William Perkin made the first synthetic material from organic chemicals in 1856. It was a purple synthetic dye he called 'mauveine'. He prepared it from a substance called aniline, which he extracted from coal tar. Coal tar is made by fiercely heating coal without air. Then the vapours given off by the hot coal are cooled. The Belgian-born chemist Leo Baekeland used a coal-tar chemical, phenol, when he produced the first synthetic plastic, Bakelite, in 1907.

Oil provides the chemicals for most synthetic products today. But coal tar will again become a major source of chemicals later this century when supplies of oil begin to run out.

Refining the crude

As it comes out of the ground, crude oil is a greenish-black sticky liquid, which by itself has limited uses. It has to be processed (refined) before it becomes useful. The first stage of processing is distillation, which sorts out the hundreds of hydrocarbon chemicals in the crude oil into different parts, or fractions, according to their boiling points.

The main fractions include our fuels: petrol (for car engines), kerosene (for jet engines), and gas oil (for diesel engines and central heating furnaces). Some of the thicker, heavier oil fractions are used for oiling, or lubricating, machines.

Cracking and refining

Other heavy oil fractions go for further processing, such as cracking. The cracking process breaks up their long, heavy molecules into short, lighter ones, which can be used in petrol, for example. Cracking also produces a mixture of gases, which other processes can turn into useful chemicals. One process is polymerisation, which does the reverse of cracking – it builds up small molecules into bigger ones.

Refinery processes extract thousands of different chemicals from petroleum, which are known as petrochemicals. One of the most important is the gas ethene (ethylene), which is the starting point for many plastics.

Marvellous METALS

Among the 90 or so chemical elements, about 70 are metals. We use most of them in one way or another. Often this usage takes the form of alloys, or mixtures, of metals. By choosing the metals carefully, metallurgists – scientists who work with metals – can create alloys with exactly the characteristics they want.

Every metal has its own unique set of properties, which suit it for different purposes. Our most important metal, iron, is suitable for making tools and building machines because it is so strong and hard. Our second most important metal, aluminium, is used for building aircraft because it is light.

We tend to think that all metals are hard, strong, shiny materials with a silvery colour. And most of them are. But a few are quite different. Sodium is a metal, but it is nearly as soft as butter and reacts vigorously with water. Nevertheless this metal still has its uses. For example, as a liquid it is used as a coolant in advanced nuclear 'breeder' reactors. It also produces the brilliant orange street lighting used in many cities.

▶▶

A false-colour electron microscope image of an alloy reveals its dense molecular structure.

Good conductors

One property all metals do have in common, however, is that they conduct (pass on) electricity. Copper is the best cheap conductor, which is why most copper is used in the electrical industry. Gold is an even better conductor; silver is the best. Gold is expensive, of course, but its superlative ability to conduct electricity makes it the best material for the conducting paths in microchips.

It is a pity that gold is so rare and expensive, because it has another important property. It resists corrosion, the name for chemical attack by all common substances. The only substance that will attack it is *aqua regia*. Meaning 'royal water', this is a mixture of the most concentrated sulphuric and nitric acids. In fact, chemicals attack most metals. Even oxygen in the air corrodes metals. Iron, for example, is attacked by oxygen and changes to the oxide we know as rust. In time, iron rusts away completely.

Alloys

Although we use more iron than any other metal, we do not use it in its pure state. When pure, it is relatively soft and weak. But it becomes much stronger and harder when we add small amounts of carbon to it. Then it becomes the alloy steel. In a similar way, adding copper and other metals to aluminium makes alloys as strong as steel. But they are much lighter.

Most metals are stronger when they are alloyed with other metals. And

by choosing the right kinds of metals, metallurgists can also change other properties. For example, they can turn iron into a metal that resists rusting by adding chromium and nickel to it. Both these metals naturally resist corrosion, and they confer this same property to the alloy they form with the iron.

We call this alloy s t a i n l e s s steel.

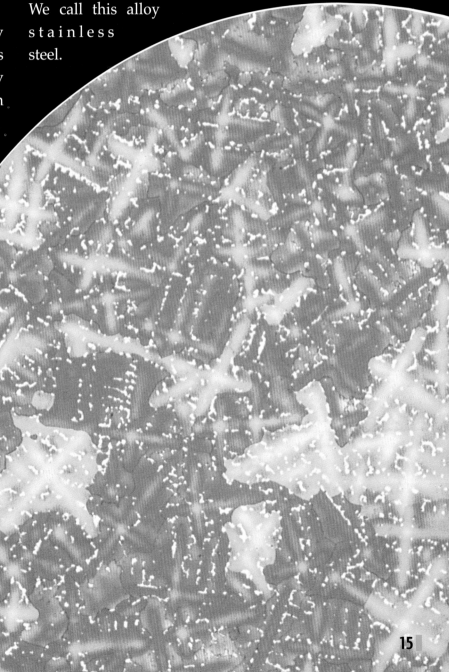

Marvellous METALS

Super alloys

The first widely used metal, bronze, is an alloy, made of copper and tin. Copper features in many other alloys, such as brass and cupronickel. Nickel is another common alloying element. One of its alloys, invar, is used in precision instruments because it does not expand or contract as the temperature changes.

An alloy of nickel and titanium, known as nitinol, is often called a memory metal because it can 'remember' its original shape after it is bent. It was developed for space equipment like antennas, which are compacted for launch and then spring into shape when they are released in space. Earthly uses for memory metals include spectacle frames, and wire for braces which gently apply pressure to straighten teeth.

Some of the most complex alloys are made by the aerospace industry for use in jet and rocket engines, which operate at very high temperatures. Called super alloys, they are combinations of what are often termed the refractory metals – heat-resistant metals with high melting points. They contain as many as 10 others, including tungsten, titanium, tantalum, niobium and molybdenum. Most have melting points between 2000–3000°C (3500–5500°F).

Superconductors

Another series of interesting alloys are used as superconductors. Ordinary metals are good conductors of electricity but still have some resistance to the flow of electric current. Superconductors have no electrical resistance at all. Once a current has been set up in these materials, it keeps flowing without the need to feed in any more electricity. Two good superconductors are niobium/germanium and niobium/titanium alloys.

Superconductors could possibly revolutionise electronics. But there is a major problem. They become superconducting only when they are cooled to very low temperatures, say, by using liquid nitrogen at –196°C (–320°F). This is very costly.

► ►

Modern methods of shaping metals include cutting with an extremely powerful laser, as shown here.

Shaping metals

Traditionally, metals are shaped in a variety of ways. In the molten state, they may be cast into shape in moulds. They can also be forged, or hammered, into shape and rolled, or squeezed between heavy rollers. Finishing touches are provided by machining, using power-driven machine tools such as lathes and drills.

For some metals, however, such shaping methods are impractical. Metals with high melting points, like tungsten, are shaped by powder metallurgy. Powdered metal is pressed into shape in a mould as it is being heated. Another powder-metal process uses explosions to compress the powder. This is called explosion forming.

Other advanced techniques that are used for shaping metals include electromagnetic forming, which uses powerful magnetic fields to shape the metal. Advanced machining processes have also been developed to work to greater precision and to cope with complex shapes. In chemical machining, for example, chemicals are used to eat away unwanted metal. Other methods use sparks, beams of electrons and lasers.

polymers and PLASTICS

Plastics gain their special properties from molecules made up of long chains of up to as many as 50,000 carbon atoms. These long chains make plastics easy to shape. Among the elements, only carbon can link with itself in this way.

▲

Chemist Leo Baekeland (1863-1944) prepared the first synthetic plastic, Bakelite, in 1907 using the chemical phenol, extracted from coal tar.

►►

Modern plastics are moulded to create hard-wearing items, such as these children's building blocks.

Molecules made up of long chains of carbon atoms are known as polymers (meaning 'many parts'). Some polymers occur naturally, in both plants and animals. The cellulose that makes up the woody tissue of plants is a polymer; so is natural rubber. Proteins such as the wool of sheep and the hair on your head are also natural polymers.

Cellulose was used to make the first plastic, celluloid. An American printer named John Hyatt invented the substance in 1869, while he was trying to find a substitute for ivory to make billiard balls. Today, celluloid is still used to make table-tennis balls – no material is better.

Synthetic polymers

Most plastics, however, are not made from natural materials like cellulose, but are mainly obtained from organic chemicals created by refining petroleum (see page 13). They are wholly synthetic. Their long-chain molecules are built up from substances with short molecules. The long molecules of the common plastic polythene (polyethene) are built up from simple short molecules of ethene (ethylene). Ethene is called the monomer ('one part'). The chemical process that makes monomers join together to form polymers is called polymerisation.

Thermoplastics and thermosets

There are hundreds of different kinds of plastics, but they divide into two main types – thermoplastics and thermosetting plastics, or thermosets. The difference between them lies in the way they behave when they are reheated. Thermoplastics – such as polythene – soften when they are reheated; thermosets – like Bakelite – do not.

This difference in the way these plastics behave is related to their molecular structure. The long molecules of thermoplastics are separate and can slide over one another as the plastic heats up and softens. The long molecules in thermosets are linked together by chemical bonds. These cross-links keep the plastic rigid no matter how much heat is applied. Eventually they will just burn.

Shaping plastics

Thermoplastics are easy to shape. For example, they can be moulded. First they are softened by heating and then injected or blown into moulds. Or they can be shaped by extrusion. In this process the molten plastic is forced through dies (shaped pieces of metal) to make tubing or through slits to make film.

Thermosets, however, have to be shaped in a different way, often by compression moulding. In this process, granules of partly formed plastic are pressed into moulds while being heated. They cross-link and set rigid as they are being shaped.

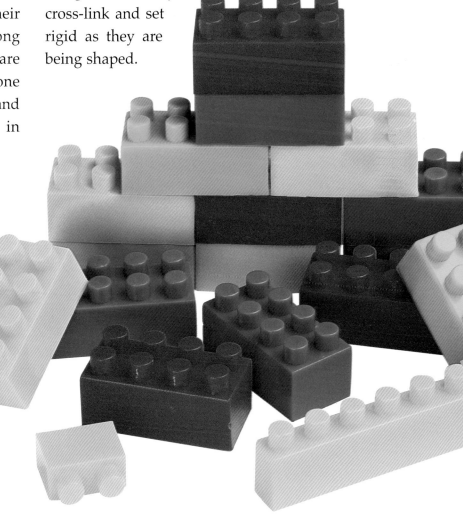

polymers and PLASTICS

Tailor-making plastics

Using many different chemical processes, scientists transform the organic chemicals obtained from oil refining into hundreds of different plastics. They can virtually tailor-make plastics with just the properties required by choosing the right basic chemical and then changing its molecules in a suitable way, such as by replacing some of its atoms with those of other elements.

Scientists can alter the conditions of manufacture to change the form plastics take. For example, they change the length of the carbon chain and keep it straight or make it branch. Long chains produce stronger materials; there is greater attraction between the molecules. Straight chains pack more tightly together, producing denser materials. Molecules with side branches are unable to pack together as tightly and so they are less dense.

PTFE, or Teflon – the world's most slippery material – coats this pan and stops food from sticking to it.

Plastic 'families'

Whole families of plastics can be obtained from similar basic chemicals, utilising their ability to form polymers. The best example is the gas ethene (ethylene, chemical formula C_2H_4). Ethene itself polymerises to form polythene, one of the first and still one of the most widely used plastics. In its high-density (long, straight-chain) form, it is made into all kinds of moulded products, from bowls to toys. Low-density (side-branched) polythene makes plastic film, which is used for carrier bags in shops, for example.

When one of ethene's hydrogen atoms is replaced by chlorine, it becomes vinyl chloride. Polymerised, this becomes the familiar plastic PVC (polyvinyl chloride). This has a host of uses such as roof guttering, cling film and designer clothing.

Ethene becomes tetrafluoroethene when all four of its hydrogen atoms are replaced with fluorine atoms. Polymerised, it becomes PTFE (polytetrafluoroethene). This is an amazing material, resistant to high temperatures and as slippery as ice. More widely known as Teflon, it provides the non-stick coating that is used on cookware.

Replace one hydrogen atom in ethene with a benzene ring (a molecule with a ring of six carbon atoms), and you get styrene. Polymerised, this becomes polystyrene, widely used in the form of foam as insulation. It also forms a hard transparent plastic.

Plastics research

Exciting things are happening all the time in plastics as chemists experiment with the cocktail of organic chemicals that come from petroleum. For example, plastics are normally good electrical insulators, but by 'doping' certain polymers with special chemicals, they can be turned into conductors of electricity. Conducting polymers can be used to make batteries, radiation shields, paints and even clothing fibres.

Work is also underway to cope with the eventual disposal of plastics, which can cause a problem because most plastics do not rot. Scientists are coming up with degradable plastics, which gradually break down. They have designed biodegradable plastics containing starch, which can be broken down by soil-dwelling bacteria. They have also designed degradable plastic thread for use by surgeons in stitching wounds. These gradually dissolve over time.

▼

This police officer in full riot gear relies on equipment made from extra-strong plastics for protection.

POPULAR PLASTICS AND THEIR USES

Plastic	Uses
Thermoplastics	
Polythene	Buckets, bowls, bottles, drums, bags
Polyvinyl chloride (PVC)	Guttering, pipes, electrical insulation, window frames, fashion wear
Polyethylene terephthalate (PET)	Carbonated drinks bottles
Polypropylene	Kitchen and bathroom fittings, transparent packaging film
Polytetrafluoroethene (PTFE)	Non-stick cookware; self-lubricating bearings
Polycarbonate	Transparent roofing sheets, see-through covers for hi-fis, etc
Polymethyl methacrylate (PMMA)	Tough transparent sheet (Perspex) for boat windshields, etc
Styrene-butadiene	Synthetic rubber used for tyres
Neoprene	Durable oil-resistant synthetic rubber
Thermosets	
Phenol-formaldehyde (Bakelite)	Moulded electrical fittings, insulation
Melamine-formaldehyde	Heat-resistant kitchen worktops, plastic tableware
Polyurethane	Foams for cavity insulation; mouldings for window frames

Fibres and COMPOSITES

Man-made fibres are now used as much as natural ones to make the clothes we wear. They are also widely used to produce strong and lightweight composite materials.

Our ancestors began using fibres to make clothing thousands of years ago, beginning with the wool of sheep. Later, fibres of cotton, linen (from the flax plant) and silk (from the silkworm) came into use. The fibres were spun into yarn, and then the yarn woven into cloth.

Today, cloth is still woven, but a much wider range of fibres is used, many man-made. They include rayon, which is made from natural cellulose. The cellulose is dissolved in chemicals, and then the solution is forced through the tiny holes of a device called a spinneret. The thin streams of solution turn into pure cellulose fibres in an acid bath.

Synthetic fibres

Most man-made fibres are now made synthetically, from petrochemicals. Synthetic fibres are kinds of plastics that can be drawn out into fine threads. The best-known and original synthetic fibre is nylon, a plastic known as a polyamide. Fibres are made by melting the plastic and forcing it through a spinneret. Polyesters and acrylics are two other common synthetic fibres. Synthetic fibres are very much stronger than natural fibres. They resist insect attack, do not rot and do not absorb water, which makes them 'drip dry'.

Some synthetic fibres have exceptional properties. One is Kevlar, which is a plastic material known as a polyaramid, related to nylon. Kevlar is very lightweight and five times stronger than steel. It is used to make bullet-proof vests for the police and military, and is also widely used in spacecraft construction. Its strength comes from the well-ordered arrangement of its polymer chains.

Another range of fibres is made by baking synthetic fibres, like acrylics. The process removes all the side atoms in the molecules and leaves just the long chains of carbon atoms. These carbon fibres are light, strong and exceptionally stiff.

Composites

Fibres of one kind or another are used increasingly to reinforce, or strengthen, materials. Typically, they are incorporated in plastics to produce materials called composites.

The material popularly known as fibreglass is the most widely used composite. It is used to make vaulting poles that can bend almost double without snapping. Fibreglass (also called GRP, glass-reinforced plastic) is also widely used to build boat hulls. A mat of glass fibres is placed on a mould, and plastic resin is applied over it. The resultant material is light, strong and does not rot.

Composites reinforced with carbon fibres are also widely used, for example, for sports equipment such as tennis racquets. Being strong and light, they also have many uses in the aerospace industry.

◄ ◄

A pole-vaulter uses a pole made from composite material. It is able to bend nearly double without breaking in two.

▼

A bullet-proof vest used by the police. It is lined with layers of Kevlar.

adhesives and superglues

Synthetic adhesives have mostly replaced natural gums and glues for joining materials together. Many are strong enough to be used in the construction of aeroplanes and spacecraft.

Sticky glues made from animal skins and bones, and pastes made from starch were among the first adhesives used. So were the gums that ooze from certain trees when the bark is cut. The rubber solution used to mend punctures in tyre inner tubes is an adhesive of this type. It is made by dissolving rubber in a solvent (dissolving substance). When the solution is applied, the solvent evaporates, leaving sticky rubber behind.

Synthetic adhesives

These days, synthetic rubber is generally used instead of natural rubber. In fact, most adhesives are now synthetic, made largely from petroleum. Some are also applied as solutions, including the polystyrene cement used in making models.

Among the strongest synthetic adhesives are the epoxy resins. They come in two parts, a partly formed plastic resin plus a curing agent. The curing agent makes the resin molecules cross-link and set rigid when the two are mixed. Epoxy adhesives are widely used not only for do-it-yourself repairs in the home but also in aerospace construction.

Similar adhesives that cure and cross-link are used to bond the heat-resistant tiles to the airframe of the space shuttle. They are based on silicone resins, which have better resistance to heat than ordinary ones. This is required because the shuttle experiences intense heat when re-entering the Earth's atmosphere. The silicone resins have atoms of heat-resistant silicon incorporated into their long-chain molecules.

Superglues

Most adhesives take time to set, but some do so instantly. Known as superglues, they are made up of acrylic resin plus a chemical called a stabiliser. In the tube, the stabiliser stops the resin polymerising into rigid plastic.

When it is applied to a surface, slight traces of moisture overcome the action of the stabiliser, and the resin turns into solid plastic in seconds. Great care must be taken when handling superglues; they stick skin together readily because skin is always slightly moist.

Gecko power

Research into adhesives often takes strange directions. One involves the study of the gecko, a lizard that can walk up walls and upside-down along ceilings. Geckos can cling to almost any surface except Teflon.

Using electron microscopes, researchers discovered that gecko feet are covered with millions of tiny hairs. Each hair creates a weak molecular bond with atoms in the surfaces on which the gecko walks. Scientists in the USA have now manufactured a prototype re-usable adhesive based on this principle.

This electron micrograph of the toes of a Tokay gecko shows the millions of tiny hairs that allow it to defy gravity and walk up walls.

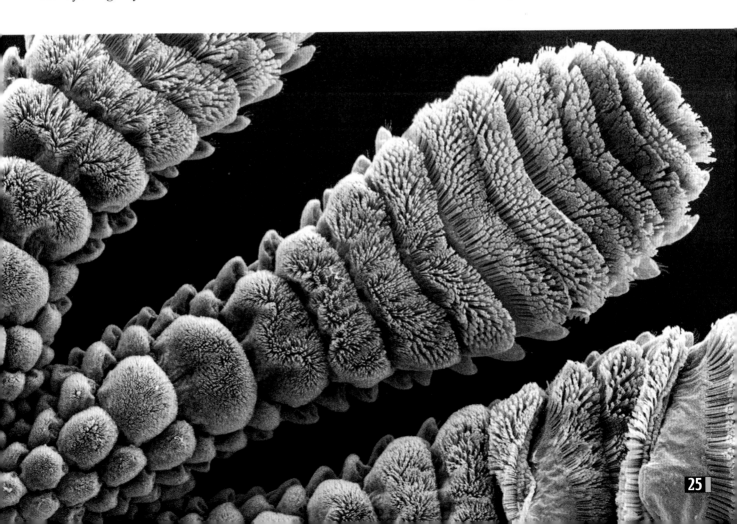

CERAMICS
AND GLASS

Ceramics are products made from earthy materials like clay and sand. Fashioned into pottery, they were among the earliest man-made materials. Today, they have a host of more specialist applications in furnaces, jet engines and spacecraft.

By moulding a mixture of clay into shape and then baking it in a kiln (furnace), you can make pottery. Ordinary pottery, called earthenware, is fired (baked) at a temperature of about 1,000°C (1,800°F). It is relatively soft and porous, and so it needs to be glazed (given a glassy coating) before it becomes watertight and useful for plates, cups and so on.

The finest pottery, porcelain, is made from purer clays and fired at temperatures of about 1,400°C (2,500°F). At such temperatures, the clays vitrify, or become glass-like. So porcelain is hard, watertight and translucent (it lets light through). Because it is an excellent insulator, porcelain is widely used in the electrical industry.

Refractories

Created in furnaces, ceramics are themselves resistant to high temperatures. Those that have exceptional heat resistance are called refractories. They are commonly used, for example, to line the furnaces in which metals are made. Furnace-linings are made from materials rich in silica (silicon dioxide) and alumina (aluminium oxide). These oxides melt only at very high temperatures. For example, alumina melts at 2,050°C/3,700°F.

There are many more specialised refractories. A common material used to make high-speed cutting tools, which need to remain strong and sharp even when red-hot, is tungsten carbide. This is a compound of carbon and tungsten, the metal with the highest melting point (3,380°C/6,120°F). The carbides of boron and silicon are also good refractories. So are the nitrides (compounds with nitrogen) of silicon and other elements.

Carbon by itself can also act as a refractory. It is used to make crucibles, containers to hold molten metals. It has an even higher melting point – 3,550°C (6,420°F) – than tungsten. Most carbon refractories are made from coke, which is produced by heating coal in the absence of air. Higher-quality refractories are made from graphite, a naturally occurring form of carbon.

Gems and chips

Those prime refractory materials – carbon, alumina and silica – are also the starting point for other interesting ceramic products. Another natural form of carbon is diamond, which is the hardest material known, natural or man-made.

By imitating the process that formed diamonds in the Earth's crust – great heat and pressure – artificial diamond can be made. So, under similar conditions, can artificial ruby. Artificial diamonds find a use in drill bits for example, while artificial ruby is used to make rods for solid lasers. Ruby lasers are the most powerful kinds of lasers and can cut metal.

Another high-tech ceramic product is the silicon from which microchips are made. It is produced by heating silica with carbon in an electric furnace.

▲

A technician shapes a piece of metal using a ruby laser. These are manufactured from rods of artificial ruby.

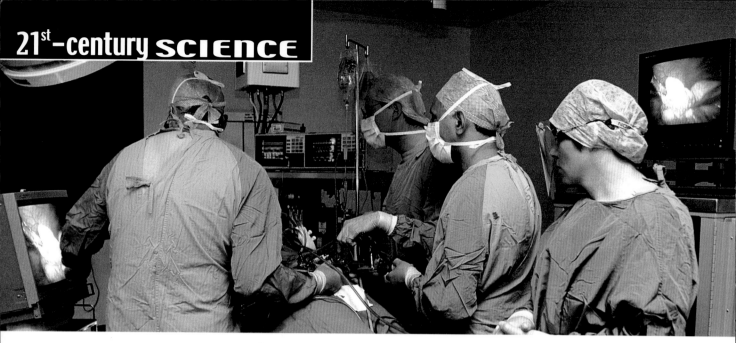

CERAMICS AND GLASS

Ceramics in aerospace

In the aerospace industry, specialist refractories called cermets are used to make jet and rocket engine parts, which need to operate at high temperatures. They combine the heat resistance of ceramics with the strength of metals. They contain ceramic materials such as tungsten, titanium and tantalum carbides and metals such as cobalt, chromium and aluminium. Because of their resistance to high temperatures, cermets cannot be shaped by normal metal-shaping processes, such as forging and casting. They have to be shaped by such techniques as powder metallurgy (see page 17).

Shuttle ceramics

Some of the most interesting refractories are used on spacecraft that return from space. These craft have to withstand the high temperatures generated by air friction when they re-enter the atmosphere. Some craft have heat shields made of what are called ablative materials. These are plastic composites (see page 23) that dissipate the heat of re-entry as they melt and boil away.

The space shuttle uses a variety of materials to protect its rather conventional airframe, which is constructed mainly from aluminium alloys. During re-entry, the shuttle orbiter experiences temperatures reaching as high as 1,500°C (2,700°F), but aluminium alloys melt at only about 700°C (1,300°F).

Much of the upper side of the orbiter, which experiences the least heating, is protected by Nomex felt, which is made of high-strength, heat-resistant fibres similar to Kevlar (see page 23). The underside, which experiences higher temperatures, is protected by ceramic tiles made out of silica fibres. Each of the 20,000 or so tiles is individually shaped exactly to fit on the airframe.

A different material is needed for the nose and leading (front) wing edges of the orbiter, which experience the highest temperatures. Called reinforced carbon-carbon (RCC), it is made from a laminate (layers) of rayon cloth, impregnated with phenolic resin. By means of strong heating, the resin is converted into carbon. Further treatment converts the upper layers into silicon carbide to stop the carbon oxidising (combining with the oxygen in the air) and weakening.

Amazing glass

Hard, transparent, resistant to all common chemicals, easy to shape and inexpensive to make, glass is a real wonder material. It is a ceramic product made by heating sand and other materials in a furnace at temperatures of about 1,500°C (2,700°F).

Altering the glass-making recipe produces different kinds of glass. For example, adding traces of metal oxides produces stained (coloured) glass. Adding boron compounds produces borosilicate glass – such as Pyrex – which is heat resistant and tough. Borosilicate glass is used widely in science and industry to make scientific apparatus and reaction vessels. Another speciality glass incorporates lead. Because it blocks radiation it is used in the nuclear industry to make windows in facilities that handle radioactive materials.

Fibres of glass provide the reinforcement in most plastic composites (page 23). Very pure glass fibres are used in the exciting field of fibre optics. These fibres transmit light by internal reflection, so that little leaks out the sides. In fibre-optic telephone cables, hair-thin fibres carry signals as beams of laser light.

A fibre-optic device allows these surgeons to see inside a patient without an invasive operation.

The space shuttle's aluminium airframe is protected from the heat of re-entry by ceramic tiles.

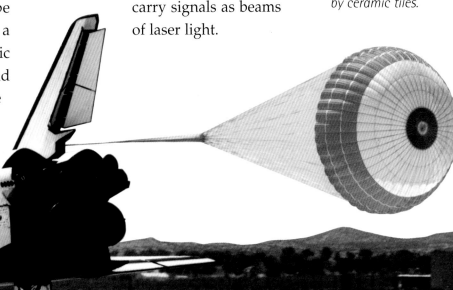

CLEVER CRYSTALS

Artificially made crystals are behind many of today's electronic miracles, such as lasers and computers. The most important of them is silicon, the substance used to make microchips.

Most of the chemical elements are either metals or non-metals. Metals conduct (pass on) electricity well. Non-metals (except carbon) do not. Some elements have properties in between metals and non-metals and are called semimetals or metalloids. They include silicon, germanium, selenium and gallium.

Silicon is the most widely used semiconductor. In its pure state, it does not conduct electricity. But when tiny amounts of impurities are added, it conducts electricity a little. It becomes a semiconductor and can be made into devices such as diodes and transistors. These devices can be incorporated in electronic circuits, where they are used to switch and amplify (strengthen) electric currents, for example in computers (see page 32).

Let there be light

Diodes are devices made up of two bits of slightly different semiconductor crystals. They will pass electric current in only one direction. Some give off light when current passes through them, and they are called light-emitting diodes (LEDs). They are widely used for digital displays in all kinds of equipment.

Another common kind of digital display uses strange liquid crystals, forming LCDs (liquid crystal displays). LCDs are also used in computer displays, such as the TFT (thin film transistor) flat screens. An LCD works because liquid crystals change their structure when charged with electricity and alter the path of light passing through them. This property is used to stop light coming out of parts of the display, which therefore show up dark.

Incredible lasers

Crystals are also used to make lasers. Artificial ruby is used to make the powerful ruby laser, which is a rod with mirrors at each end. Energy is pumped into the ruby rod and excites (gives extra energy to) some of its atoms. These atoms give off the extra energy as radiation.

This radiation then stimulates (triggers) other atoms into giving off radiation, which is reflected back and forth by the mirrored ends. The radiation builds up and eventually emerges from one end as an intense beam of very pure light.

The word laser comes from the process that produces laser light – light amplification by stimulated emission of radiation.

Semiconductor materials are also used to make lasers. In CD players semiconductor lasers produce the beam that reads the discs. This type of laser also changes voice signals into pulses of light in fibre-optic telecommunications.

▲

Not all lasers cut metal - a beam of laser light marks the Prime Meridian of longitude at Greenwich in London.

SUPER SILICON

Silicon, one of the commonest elements in the Earth's crust, is used not only to make 'chips' for computers, but also devices like solar cells and CCDs.

The silicon chips used for the processing of circuits and memories in computers consist largely of electronic components called transistors. These devices act as switches to let current flow or not flow through circuits. The flow or non-flow of electricity represents the two states of the binary (two-digit) code on which computers operate – 1 and 0.

Transistors are made up of three different pieces of semiconductor material sandwiched together – usually two n-type semiconductors with a p-type in between. N-type material has a few extra electrons, while p-type has a few 'holes' through which electrons from the n-type material can flow.

Shrinking circuits

Transistors came into widespread use in the 1950s. They were much smaller and more robust than the valves (vacuum tubes) they replaced. This led, for example, to pocket-sized transistor radios. At first, transistors were used as separate devices in circuits. But in 1958 whole circuits containing transistors and other electronic components (diodes, resistors, capacitors) were incorporated into a single component.

These integrated circuits greatly reduced the size of electronic equipment. Today, in large-scale integration, millions of electronic components can be incorporated into a single silicon wafer, or chip. It is called a microchip because the circuits can be seen only under a microscope. Chips called microprocessors can now contain the complete circuits of a computer.

Many stages are needed to make a silicon chip. The starting point is a slice of pure silicon. Then various layers of different materials (n- and p-type) are built up step by step, by a series of masking, etching and doping operations – treatment with certain chemicals, such as phosphorus and boron. Several hundred chips are made at a time from a circular silicon slice about 10 cm (4 in) across.

Solar cells and CCDs

These two kinds of devices, which react to light, are also based on silicon. A solar cell is a two-layer sandwich of n-type and p-type semiconductor. When light hits the junction between the two, through the near transparent upper n-type layer, electricity is produced.

Panels made up of thousands of these solar, or photovoltaic, cells power space satellites.

A CCD, or charge-coupled device, consists of an array (pattern) of light-sensitive units, or picture elements (pixels). They store the pattern of light falling on them as a pattern of electric charges, which can be 'read' and stored as an electronic image. CCDs are used in video and digital cameras.

▼
This picture shows two circular slices of silicon with hundreds of microchips on each.

Hydrogen, the most plentiful substance in the universe, could hold the key to the world's future energy needs. Scientists believe it could be used in the short term in fuel cells; and in the long term in nuclear fusion reactors, using the same process that keeps the stars shining in the heavens.

fuels
for the future

Most of the energy the world uses today comes from the fossil fuels – petroleum (oil), natural gas and coal. These fuels have formed over hundreds of millions of years, and once they have been used up they cannot be replaced. Burning these fuels, in our cars and electric power stations, also produces fumes that pollute our atmosphere and adds to global warming.

For powering vehicles, various kinds of substitute fuels have been tried. They include gasahol, which is a mixture of petrol (gasoline) and alcohol. The alcohol can be obtained cheaply by fermenting corn (maize) wastes. Refined oil from the seeds of rape plants has proved to be an effective substitute for diesel fuel for heavier vehicles.

Electric power

A return to electric cars is also being made. These were popular a century ago when cars powered by petrol engines were in their infancy. They have the advantage over ordinary cars of producing no fumes and no pollution. The 'old-technology' electric cars used batteries to power the motors that drove their wheels. The batteries were kept charged from mains electricity.

The 'new technology' cars are powered by fuel cells, the same power source that the space shuttle uses. Such cells combine hydrogen with oxygen to produce electricity. Hydrogen is easy to produce by passing an electric current through water, in a process called electrolysis. Then, the two gases combine to produce harmless water.

Power forever

For the large scale generation of power, renewable resources like hydroelectric, solar and wind power will become increasingly important as supplies of the fossil fuels dwindle. But they cannot possibly produce enough power for the world.

More nuclear power, using the nuclear fission (splitting) of uranium atoms, would be one way of maintaining energy production. But most countries are against this because of the dangers of radiation from damaged reactors and nuclear wastes.

But there is a different kind of nuclear power that could supply the world's energy needs forever. This uses the nuclear fusion (joining together) of hydrogen atoms. Nuclear fusion is the process that keeps the Sun and the stars shining. The fusion of hydrogen produces fantastic amounts of energy but no dangerous radiation. And there is enough hydrogen in the oceans to last the world indefinitely.

◄ ◄
A close-up view of the thousands of circuits on a computer microchip.

▼
This solar-powered telephone in Australia helps people in remote areas to keep in touch.

manipulating molecules AND genes

Scientists and engineers can now tinker with the tiniest bits of materials – molecules – in the search for new and better materials. Genetic engineers can even swap the genes in living things, changing the way they grow and behave.

All the different substances and materials on Earth are made up of tiny molecules. In turn, the molecules are made up of a number of atoms combined together. Using the latest techniques, scientists can now see and even move individual atoms. This became possible following the invention of the scanning tunnelling microscope in the 1980s.

Scientists can use this microscope to pick up and move atoms around to create different molecules that have interesting properties. For example, they have created molecules shaped like propellers, which spin when they are heated. One day these could become the heart of motors as tiny as grains of pollen. The development of such tiny molecular devices is known as nanotechnology. It is so called because it works with atoms, which measure only nanometres (billionths of a metre) across.

Molecular modelling

Finding the precise structure of biological molecules is of vital importance in medicine. Medical researchers now use powerful computers to help them unravel molecular structures. They feed information about the chemical make-up of, say, a virus into the computer, which is programmed with all the rules that govern how the different atoms in the substance can link up. The computer then comes up with a probable structure.

The researchers then use the

computer to design new drugs or vaccines with a molecule suitably shaped to fit round the virus. And this should prevent the virus doing its deadly work.

Genetic engineering

Arguably the most important molecule of all is DNA (deoxyribose nucleic acid). This is the 'molecule of life' found in the cells of living things, which contains all the information needed by a living organism to grow and reproduce. It carries units called genes, which determine the nature and behaviour of the organism.

Scientists can now remove the genes from one organism and insert them into the DNA of others. This kind of work is called genetic engineering. Using this technique, scientists have produced bacteria that make human insulin to treat diabetes. They have produced tomatoes that stay ripe longer without softening, potatoes that produce a toxin that poisons insect pests, and maize (corn) that is resistant to weed killers. But the development of such GM (genetically modified) foods is controversial because of the possibility that the introduced genes will 'escape' and harm the natural environment.

Oil pressed from the seeds of genetically modified rape plants – shown here – is likely to become an important new raw material.

materials in SPACE

Scientists make use of the unique weightless conditions that exist in orbiting spacecraft to gain a greater insight into the structure and behaviour of different substances. This could result in a whole range of new materials, from stronger alloys to more effective anti-cancer drugs.

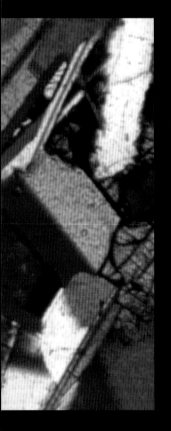

In an orbiting spacecraft, everything appears weightless. It seems that gravity no longer exists, although this isn't really true. Weightlessness comes about because of the way the spacecraft speeds round the Earth.

Space scientists call this apparent weightless condition micro-gravity. They have been investigating a range of materials in space experiments since the time of the first successful space station, Skylab, in 1973. Experiments continued on the space shuttle and in the space laboratory Spacelab, on the Salyut and Mir space stations, and will be a feature of work on the International Space Station now being built.

Growing crystals

Much work has centred on the growth of crystals in micro-gravity. On Earth, gravity distorts the way crystals grow when a liquid freezes. In metals and alloys, the distortion in crystal growth can lead to defects and weakness. In micro-gravity, the crystals can grow larger and develop without flaws. This results in a much stronger material.

Among the benefits that will come from this work are superstrong alloys, high-temperature resistant ceramics, more efficient semiconductors and better superconductors.

Other crystal-growth experiments take place in biological space research. Under investigation are different proteins, which are among the building blocks of living things. Micro-gravity provides the conditions in which perfectly shaped protein crystals can be obtained.

From these perfect crystals, the precise structure of the proteins can be determined. This holds the key to understanding how they function and how they might be controlled and altered. This could lead to the design

spacecraft stays in orbit. Damage caused by space hazards could limit the life of orbiting structures like space stations. Experiments carried out on the early space stations and special satellites like the LDEF (long-duration exposure facility) have shown that materials do deteriorate

of better antibiotics and more effective drugs to combat deadly viruses like AIDS and treat cancerous tumours.

Space exposure

Another aspect of materials in space is the effect on them of exposure to the space environment. This becomes increasingly important the longer a

in space. Plastics, which are widely used in spacecraft, tend to erode (wear away) and weaken. Metals can become radioactive because of exposure to cosmic rays. And all structures are subjected to continuous bombardment by the swarms of meteoroids (tiny rock particles) present in space.

▲

A micrograph of a cross-section of Moon rock shows its amazing crystalline structure.

CONSERVATION and RECYCLING

Every year billions of tonnes of minerals and petroleum are dug, blasted or pumped out of the ground in mining operations to provide the raw materials our world needs. Sooner or later supplies of these materials will run out.

First the good news. Supplies of iron ores to make our most important metal, steel, are plentiful, and will last for several hundred years. Supplies of aluminium ores are also plentiful. But many of our other important metals, including copper, silver, gold, tin, lead, tungsten and platinum, could run out within the next 50 years.

Substitutes can be found for some of these scarce metals, and advances in technology may help relieve the pressure on others. For instance, fibre-optic cables, made of hair-like strands of glass, are increasingly replacing copper cables in communications (page 29). And electronic, filmless photography is reducing the demand for silver, whose salts are key chemicals in photographic film. In digital cameras, pictures are taken in the form of electronic images on CCD chips (page 33).

Recycling

To put off the day when mineral supplies will run out, it is essential that we re-use, or recycle materials when we can. Scrap metal has been collected and recycled on a small scale for many years, but the practice is now becoming more widespread.

Old cars provide a major source of scrap for the iron and steel industry. Drinks cans are widely recycled for the aluminium industry. Recycling aluminium is important not only for conserving the metal, but also for conserving energy. It takes about twenty times the energy to extract aluminium from its ore than it does to extract from scrap. The same argument applies to recycling glass – a lot of energy is required to make glass from its plentiful main raw material, sand. So once again, recycling makes sense.

The fossil fuels

As with minerals, there are only limited amounts of fossil fuels in the Earth's crust. And we are fast using them up. They are important not just as fuels, but as raw materials for the chemical industry (page 12).

Petroleum may begin to run out in the middle of this century. Then the chemical industry will have to switch back to processing coal into chemicals. Fortunately there is enough coal available in the Earth's crust to last for centuries.

Nevertheless, if we can recycle chemical products, so much the better. Plastics account for a large part of chemical production, and they are now being recycled on a large scale in many countries.

In processing, plastics are heated in the absence of air. They decompose to form vapours, which are condensed into liquid chemicals in distillation columns. The chemicals can then be used to manufacture new products, so beginning the materials cycle once more.

▲

Recycling will play an increasingly important part in everyday life in the 21st century.

◀ ◀

Materials await recycling at a civic facility.

GLOSSARY

adhesive
A substance used to join materials.

alloy
A mixture of metals, or of a metal and another chemical element.

CCD (charge-coupled device)
An electronic device used in digital cameras to capture an image.

ceramics
Products made by baking earthy materials.

composite
A material usually made of plastic, reinforced with fibres.

compound
A substance formed by the chemical combination of different elements.

conductor
A material that conducts electricity.

corrosion
The process that attacks and breaks down metals.

cracking
A process that breaks down heavier oil fractions into lighter ones.

doping
Treating a silicon chip with chemical vapour to change its electrical state.

elements
The basic chemical 'building blocks' that make up all matter.

fibreglass
A composite material of plastics reinforced with glass fibres.

fibre optics
The branch of science and technology concerned with the transmission of light through optical fibres, as in the telecommunications industry.

hydrocarbon
A compound made up of hydrogen and carbon only.

laser
A device that produces an intense beam of very pure light.

metallurgy
The science and technology of metals.

microchip
A silicon chip that contains electronic circuits of microscopic size.

mineral
A chemical compound found in the ground.

nanotechnology
A branch of science concerned with the manipulation of materials on an atomic scale.

ore
A mineral from which metal can profitably be extracted.

petrochemical
A chemical obtained by refining petroleum.

petroleum
Crude oil, as it comes from the ground.

plastic
A synthetic material made up of long-chain molecules.

pollution
The poisoning of the land, water, air and the environment in general.

polymer
A substance with long molecules; polymerisation is the process by which polymers and plastics are made.

rayon
A man-made fibre made from natural cellulose.

recycling
Using materials again and again.

refining
In metallurgy, removing impurities from metals; in the oil industry, processing petroleum into useful products.

refractory
A material that resists high temperatures.

semiconductor
A substance that conducts electricity a little under certain conditions.

silicon chip
A thin wafer of 'doped' silicon containing miniaturised electronic circuits.

smelting
The process of heating ore in a furnace to extract metal.

solar cell
A cell that produces electricity from sunlight.

superconductor
A material that has no electrical resistance.

super alloy
A complex alloy for high-temperature or high-stress use, for example in jet aircraft engines.

synthetics
Materials made wholly from chemicals.

thermoplastics
Plastics that re-melt when heated.

thermosets
Plastics that do not re-melt when heated.

transistor
A semiconductor device that forms one of the essential components in silicon chips.

21ˢᵗ-century SCIENCE

INDEX

A

adhesives 24-25, 42
alloys 8, 9, 14, 15, 16, 28, 38, 42
aluminium 14, 15, 26, 28, 29, 40
atoms 18, 20, 21, 23, 24, 25, 31, 35, 36

B

Baekeland, Leo 13, 18
Bakelite 13, 18, 19, 21
bronze 8, 16

C

carbon 10, 13, 15, 18, 20, 21, 23, 26, 27, 28, 29, 30, 42
cellulose 18, 22, 32, 43
ceramics 26-28, 38, 42
CCD (charge-coupled device) 33, 40, 42
chemicals 8, 10, 11, 12, 13, 14, 15, 17, 20, 22, 29, 32, 40, 41, 43
    organic 13, 18, 20, 21
chemical elements 10, 14-15, 16, 18, 26, 30, 42
coal 12, 13, 26, 34, 41
coal tar 13, 18
composite materials 22-23, 28, 29, 43
computers 30, 31, 32, 33, 36, 37

copper 14, 15, 16, 40
conductors 14, 21, 30, 42
conservation 9, 40-41

D

DNA (deoxyribose nucleic acid) 37
diamond 27

E

electricity 14, 16, 21, 30, 32, 33, 35, 42, 43
ethene 13, 18, 20, 21

F

fibre, man-made 22-23, 43
    natural 22-23
fibreglass 23, 42
fibre optics 29, 31, 40, 42
fossil fuel 12, 34-35, 41
fuel cells 34, 35

G

gas 10, 11, 12, 13, 34
genes 36, 37
glass 29, 40
gold 8, 14, 40

H

hydrocarbon 13, 42
hydrogen 10, 12, 20, 21, 34-35, 42,

I

Industrial Revolution 8

iron 8, 10, 11, 14, 15, 40

L

laser 17, 27, 29, 30, 31, 42
LED (light-emitting diodes) 30
LCD (liquid crystal display) 30

M

materials
    in space 9, 38-39
    raw 8-9, 10-11, 37, 40-41
    synthetic 8, 12-13, 43
metals 8-11, 12, 14-17, 26, 27, 28, 29, 30, 31, 38, 39, 40, 42, 43
microchips 14, 27, 30, 32, 33, 35, 42
minerals 8, 9, 10-11, 12, 40, 41, 42
molecules 13, 14, 18, 19, 20, 21, 23, 24, 36-37, 43

N

nanotechnology 36
nickel 10, 11, 14, 15, 16
nuclear fusion 34-35

O

oil 11, 12, 13, 20, 34, 42, 43
oxygen 10, 11, 15, 29, 35

P

petrochemical 13, 23, 43
petroleum 12-13, 18, 21, 24, 34, 40, 41, 43
plastics 8, 11, 12, 13, 18-21, 23, 25, 28, 29, 39, 41, 42, 43
polymers 18-21, 23, 32, 43

R

radiation 29, 31, 35
recycling 9, 40-41, 43
refractory 16, 26-28, 43
resin 24-25, 29
rocks 8-9, 10-11, 12
ruby, artificial 27, 31

S

semiconductor 30-33, 38, 43
silica 26, 27, 29
silicon 8, 24, 26, 27, 29, 30, 32-33, 42, 43
silver 8, 11, 14, 40
spacecraft 16, 23, 24, 26, 28, 29, 35, 38-39
steel 8, 15, 23, 40
superconductor 16, 43
superglue 8, 24-25

T U V

thermoplastics 19, 43
thermosets 19, 43
transistors 32, 43

These are the lists of contents for each title in *21st-Century Science*:

Energy

Our need for energy • Sources of energy • Electricity supply • Fossil fuels • Nuclear energy • Wind energy • Geothermal energy • Solar energy • Hydropower • Energy from the oceans • Biomass energy • Hydrogen and fuel cells • Energy efficiency • Energy for the future

Medicine

The living machine • Breakdowns in the body • The body under attack Fighting back • Battling bacteria • Coping with cancer • Complementary medicine • Tools of the trade • Surgery • The genetic revolution • Life in vitro • Medicine in space

Genetics

All about genetics • Chromosomes • DNA • Genes at work • Life begins • Inheriting genes • When genes go wrong • Changing DNA • Gene-splicing • Plant genetics • Mixing animal DNA • Cloning • How will we use genetics? • Genetic mysteries

Telecoms

The pace of change • Signals, senders and receivers • Wires, fibres and aerials • Multiplexing • Networks • Computer networks • Terrestrial communications • Freedom from wires • Cellular mobiles • Satellite communications • The Internet • Broadcasting • The future

Electronics

The world goes electronic • Circuits and signals • Computer building blocks • Memory • Microprocessors • CPU logic • Chip design • Making a chip • Circuit boards • Electronic sound • Displays • Sending signals • Flying electronics • The future of electronics

New materials

Raw materials • Metals • Polymers and plastics • Fibres and composites • Adhesives and superglues • Ceramics and glass • Clever crystals • Silicon • Fuels for the future • Manipulating molecules and genes • Materials in space • Conservation and recycling